LITTLE CASTLE

orecourt Stonewalk Fountain garden

Model of
Little Castle

*B*olsover Castle h̶̶ ̶
visitors for four ̶
today is its unlikely position: perched high over a
motorway, on the site of a medieval castle, in the midst
of a former coal-mining area. Another fascination of
these unique buildings is that, since they were built,
they have been relatively little
changed to suit the needs of
succeeding centuries. This is
particularly true of the Little
Castle of which the historian,
Mark Girouard, wrote: 'by an
unlikely miracle the keep at
Bolsover has survived into
this century as an almost
untouched expression in stone of the lost world of
Elizabethan chivalry and romances'.

The Little Castle is perhaps the most unusual part
of Bolsover, begun by Charles Cavendish in 1612 as
a fantasy house for leisure and lavish entertaining.
Contrasting with this tower-house of tightly stacked
rooms is the Terrace Range – a long sequence of
imposing state rooms stretching out along the ridge.
Charles's son, William, completed the remarkable
interior of the Little Castle after his father died, and
was responsible for most of the Terrace Range, including
the last phase of building here in the 1660s. He also
added the impressive Riding House buildings, to
serve his obsession with horses.

The astonishing buildings at Bolsover aroused the
curiosity of King Charles I who, in 1634, was treated
here to one of the most extravagant entertainments
of the time.

This guidebook offers a comprehensive
tour, including an explanation of the
1999/2000 conservation work. There
is also a colourful history, telling the
story of the owners of the castle
and the opulent life that was
lived here.

THE GREAT COURT

The skeleton of a dog discovered in the Great Court at Bolsover

The Great Court, showing the Little Castle and Terrace Range. The wall around the garden lies on the line of the medieval castle's inner bailey

Entering Bolsover from the south, you pass low earth banks in the playing fields by the road. These banks form the outermost defences of the medieval town that once lay on the hilltop near the Castle.

Behind the recently-built visitor centre, a similar bank surrounds the grassy Outer Court. This was the outer defence of the medieval castle which would have had several defensive walls enclosing courtyards of increasing degrees of security, one inside the other. The outer defences enclosed a bailey for timber service buildings and livestock. Outside the bank was a deep ditch, now filled in. When the visitor centre was built, the remains of a medieval building was discovered. Its roof was supported by a row of timber columns, and their bases left holes which survive in the bedrock.

Go down the drive into the Great Court. To your right, just inside the gate, is a model that shows the Castle as it was when complete in the 1660s. This entrance was actually the back door of the Castle in the seventeenth century. The formal approach was along the south drive which you will visit later. The Great Court was probably the middle bailey of the medieval castle. A medieval burial of about twenty bodies was found in the centre of the court, perhaps the result of a plague or an attack on the castle, and human remains have also been found all over the site.

THE CAVENDISH FAMILY AND THE BUILDING OF THE CASTLE

Bolsover Castle was granted as a reward by King Edward VI in 1553 to George Talbot, sixth Earl of Shrewsbury. The Earl was already a great landowner, and his country houses dominated the Midlands: his principal residence was Sheffield Castle, but he also owned Worksop Manor and Wingfield Manor. In 1568 he increased his power further when he allied his great estates, by marriage, with those of the famous Bess of Hardwick. Bess came from a family of minor gentry who were sheepfarmers at Hardwick, but she inherited large landholdings from her three previous husbands, one of whom was the courtier, William Cavendish.

Bess had had eight children by William, and the Earl had several children from a previous marriage. When Bess and the Earl of Shrewsbury married, two of Bess's children married two of the Earl's – a merger that sealed the business interests of their families. However, Bess and the Earl quarrelled over land and money, and Bess retreated to the house that she had built at Hardwick. In spite of this rift, the fortunes of the two families were to remain closely linked because, as well as being step-brothers and brothers- in-law, Bess's youngest son Charles,

and the Earl's son Gilbert, became close friends. When the sixth Earl died in 1590, and Gilbert became the seventh Earl, he sought to increase the family fortunes by first leasing and then selling Welbeck Abbey and the ruins of Bolsover Castle to Charles.

BUILDING A NEW CASTLE

It seems likely that Charles worked with the famous builder and designer, Robert Smythson, who had brilliantly designed Hardwick Hall for his mother. Smythson is credited with the design of many other fine houses, including Longleat in Wiltshire and Wollaton Hall in Nottingham (see page 33). Both Charles Cavendish and Robert Smythson were to die before work had proceeded

very far at Bolsover – Smythson in 1614 and Cavendish in 1617 – and the work was continued by their sons, William and John, who incorporated new ideas based on the Italian-influenced work of Inigo Jones in London. However, it is Charles Cavendish and Robert Smythson who are usually credited with the romantic concept of the Little Castle. The Terrace Range reflects the greater formality of the later seventeenth century. When John Smithson died in 1634 (he preferred, the alternative spelling of their name) it is thought that a third generation of the family - his son Huntingdon, who is buried at the Parish church - probably took over the supervision of the building works. Huntingdon Smithson may have been responsible for the bold design of the Riding House.

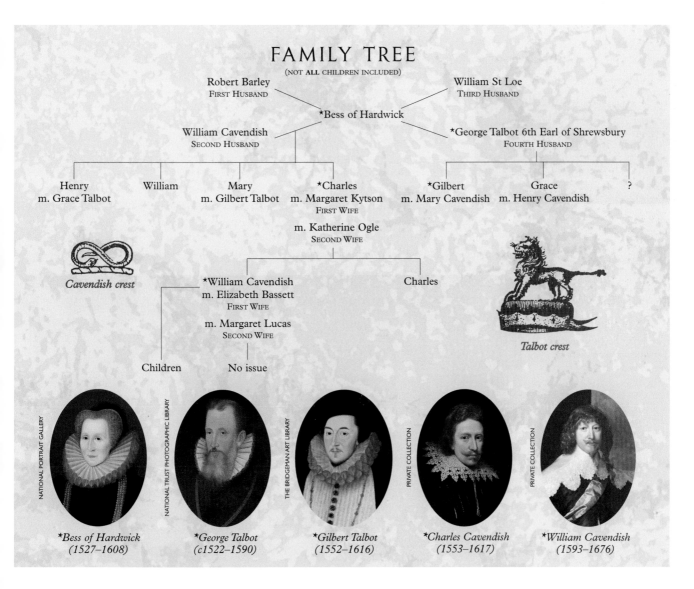

FAMILY TREE
(NOT ALL CHILDREN INCLUDED)

Robert Barley
FIRST HUSBAND

William St Loe
THIRD HUSBAND

*Bess of Hardwick

William Cavendish
SECOND HUSBAND

*George Talbot 6th Earl of Shrewsbury
FOURTH HUSBAND

Henry
m. Grace Talbot

William

Mary
m. Gilbert Talbot

*Charles
m. Margaret Kytson
FIRST WIFE

*Gilbert
m. Mary Cavendish

Grace
m. Henry Cavendish

?

m. Katherine Ogle
SECOND WIFE

Cavendish crest

*William Cavendish
m. Elizabeth Bassett
FIRST WIFE

Charles

m. Margaret Lucas
SECOND WIFE

Children

No issue

Talbot crest

Bess of Hardwick
(1527–1608)

George Talbot
(c1522–1590)

Gilbert Talbot
(1552–1616)

Charles Cavendish
(1553–1617)

William Cavendish
(1593–1676)

THE RIDING HOUSE RANGE

'An obedience place for a horse', John Smithson's design for a horse jump, 1623

ABOVE: The exterior of the Riding House, with the shoeing house to the left and the stable to the right

RIGHT: The interior of the Riding House: William Cavendish's viewing gallery was inserted into the end wall in the 1660s so that he could sit and look down on his horses in action

OPPOSITE William Cavendish is shown here on horseback performing the manoeuvre of 'Balottades par la Droite' with the Little Castle in the background. The illustration comes from his book on horsemanship

From the outside, the range of buildings with the Riding House at its centre forms an impressive long block completely enclosing the south side of the Great Court. It was built in the 1630s, entirely for William Cavendish's horses, and is an extraordinary monument to the seriousness with which Cavalier courtiers viewed their horsemanship (see pages 6 and 7). The building is in four parts, from left to right: the forge area (including the 'shooing' house), the Riding House, the stable and then an accommodation block on the end (now the toilets). The central part of the three main sections is the Riding House itself, with its gargantuan stone doorway forming a spectacular entrance. Over these buildings was accommodation possibly for grooms and the Master of the Horses. This whole range of buildings was carefully designed to align with other major features of the site. The buildings were planned so that when you stand outside the main Riding House doorway, there is a clear view straight ahead through the archway of the Fountain Garden towards the central balcony of the Little Castle, and another view (to your left) through the main entrance door of the Terrace Range and out over the Terrace.

Take the second door along the Riding House Range to enter the shoeing house and then move on through the doorway into the Riding House

RIDING HOUSE INTERIOR

The huge interior of the central Riding House remains intact, and is the finest surviving example in England of this rare, specialised type of building. The great oak roof would have originally been hidden by a ceiling. It was repaired in the

Monseigneur le Marquis
a Cheval.

Balottades par le Droite.

P. Clouet sculp

eighteenth century and again in the nineteenth, when the decorative wooden pendants in the centre were added and the ceiling removed. The three-part design of the stone viewing gallery window shows the influence of the Italian designs used widely at Bolsover – a style made famous by Palladio in northern Italy.

This huge room was not used for learning to ride, but for the art of manège: making horses circle, leap or kneel, like the famous white stallions of the Spanish Riding School in Vienna. This art was popular among fashionable gentlemen, many of whom went to study at the master de Pluvinel's Academy in Paris.

The floor had soft sand for the horses' hoofs, and the horses were tied to tall posts to train them to move round in tighter and tighter circles. The viewing gallery was added as William grew too old to ride and had to watch his servant Captain Mazine training his horses instead.

Leave the Riding House by its main door. If you wish to take a closer look at its roof, retrace your steps along the outside of the Range to the first door, where you can enter and climb the stairs to the viewing gallery.

THE STABLES

What is now the Discovery Centre was originally a stable. The horses lived in stalls twelve feet in length, arranged in a row along the wall opposite the huge door.

The room was altered after William's death. The inserted windows, the chunky plaster cornice and the triangular fireplaces were all added when the stable was made into two grand suites of rooms. Later still, the building lost its roof and was used as a cart shed and a pig sty.

A plan made by John Smithson for the new stable block he designed for Welbeck Abbey, William Cavendish's main house. The stalls at Bolsover must have been laid out in a similar way

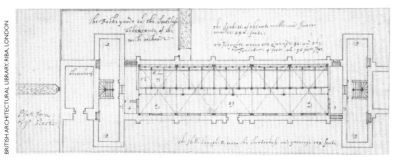

The splendid building range joining the Riding House Range at right angles, and stretching down towards the Little Castle, is the Terrace Range.

WILLIA

When William Cavendish left Cambridge University, where he had shown that he would never shine in the academic world, his father sent him to train in horsemanship at the Royal Mews. William was a similar age to James I's son Prince Henry, and when Henry's grandfather, the king of France, sent over a master to teach the prince to ride, William also attended Monsieur St Antoine's lessons. They sometimes took place in the royal riding houses at the Palaces of St James and Richmond.

Later, William was engaged as tutor to Prince Charles (who became King Charles II), and his proudest achievement was teaching the prince to ride.

William took his riding seriously, and met some criticism for it. 'They think it is a disgrace for a gentleman to do anything well. What! Be a rider. Why not?' he wrote in the introduction to his book about manège. 'I am so tormented about my book of horsemanship as you cannot believe',

Charles I, depicted on horseback by Van Dyck. He is accompanied by Monsieur St Antoine, the royal riding master who also taught William Cavendish

VENDISH AND THE ART OF MANÈGE

he wrote in 1656, two years before his book was published. He need not have worried. The book, *La Méthode Nouvelle et Invention Extraordinaire de dresser les Chevaux*, became a classic and was reprinted many times.

A list of names of 54 of William's horses survives in his own handwriting. His stable included a 'grey leaping horse, the most beautiful I ever saw' and horses from Barbary and Turkey. The most expensive was Le Superbe.

LEFT: Reconstruction drawing by Andy Gammon of a horseman riding through the grand doorway of the Riding House in the seventeenth century

BELOW: This illustration from William's horsemanship book shows William training his horses in the Riding House

THE TERRACE RANGE

The building of the Terrace Range, in the 1630s, was a result of William Cavendish's ambition to obtain a royal appointment. A contemporary wrote of him that a 'foolish ambition of glorious slavery carried him to Court, where he ran himself much in to debt, to purchase neglects of the King and Queen and scorns of the proud Courtiers'. He became a Viscount, then Earl, then Lord Lieutenant of the county. He had hoped – but failed – to be made the king's Master of the Horse. He needed a grand house to support his position, and to which he could even invite the king and queen themselves, and with this in mind, the building of the stately Terrace Range was begun.

THE BUILDING OF THE TERRACE RANGE

The story of the building of the Terrace Range is quite complicated because it was carried out in at least four stages.

Firstly, in the second decade of the seventeenth century, at the same time as the Little Castle was being built, the northern or right-hand end of the Terrace Range was converted from the remains of an older house. This accounts for its unusual slant. The basement of the Terrace Range was designed to match that of the Little Castle, having similar vaults and pillars.

The second stage of building consisted of a long gallery and great chamber, stretching out along the ridge, according to a plan made by John Smithson. On the other side of these buildings, you will notice how the windows and lines of stonework change as the builders worked southwards, adding the new gallery.

Thirdly, the earlier Great Hall was given the extra storey and curved gables that you see today. The curved gables, which replaced its flat battlemented roof, were an up-to-date, Dutch design sketched in London in 1618 by John Smithson.

Finally, in the 1660s, when William Cavendish returned from exile abroad to a neglected Bolsover, the state rooms (those you enter first) were rebuilt to designs by Samuel Marsh. The flat battlemented top of the building, and the elaborate Baroque window surrounds date from this period. These rooms provided the stateliness needed for the increasingly formal aristocratic lifestyle developing towards the end of the seventeenth century.

Approach the main entrance to the Terrace Range

OPPOSITE: The grand 1660s entrance to the Terrace Range. The 'great columes' on either side of the door are mentioned in some notes by their designer, Samuel Marsh

BELOW: A plan by John Smithson for the Terrace Range, as it was before the 1660's remodelling. The chapel to the far right was never actually built

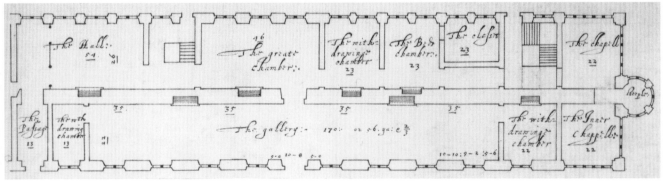

This reconstruction by Andy Gammon shows William Cavendish welcoming his son Henry and grandson Harry to the newly finished entrance hall in the 1660s

The splendid doorway from the Great Court is flanked by two monolithic columns carved from single blocks of stone. The great coat-of-arms above, marked William's elevation to the Dukedom: it is the 'creast exsteriordenarie,' brought to the house in a special carriage in the 1660s.

Walk through the doorway into the entrance hall of the building.

ENTRANCE HALL

This room contained a picture of William Cavendish in armour, on horseback, 'in full p(ro)portion'.

All our information about the furnishing of the rooms comes from notes made in 1710 by Bassano, a visiting herald.

Over the wooden rail to the right, you can see the service rooms in the basement, but have to imagine the great hall which lay above them.

If you wish to explore the service rooms and kitchens, return to the main entrance, turn left and then immediate left down some steps into the basement.

View down into the service rooms, as they are today

DINING ROOM

In the 1630s, this was part of the processional route through the house. Visitors entered at the far or lower end of the hall. If they were important enough, they passed along its full length, towards us, through a lobby, and into what was then called the 'Great Chamber', which stood where we are now. This was a chamber for the lord to eat in, away from the servants in the hall. Later the hall was remodelled as a private dining room. There was a widening gap between master and servants, and the family appropriated the hall for their own use.

Turn to face the opposite (south) end of the Terrace Range

The doorways are aligned so that you can see the rooms leading away in a line, one after another. This was meant to emphasise the large number of rooms and to show their hierarchy of increasing status. Sir Henry Wotton, the contemporary architectural writer, criticised this fashion on the grounds that it caused draughts, and served no purpose other than to show off all the furniture at once. But at nearby Chatsworth, the designer even placed a mirror on the end wall to make the suite seem twice as long.

Walk through the door into the withdrawing room.

WITHDRAWING ROOM

This room was hung with family portraits and two pictures of Charles II. These pictures were by two of the best artists of the time: Van Dyck, to whom William sent affectionate letters, and the Dutch landscape painter, Hendrick van Steenwyck. Gentlemen used portraits as a sign of their family's importance. This outward sign of status was probably of particular significance to William because the Cavendishes were not one of the old ruling families – they had come into their wealth and comparative power only recently, a fact that probably caused William to feel insecure about his position.

Continue to walk southwards until you reach the end.

LODGING ROOM

The climax of the suite of rooms was the bedroom, which was very grand. It may seem odd that a room for sleeping was the most sumptuous, but, as the term 'lodging room' implies, the bedroom of a nobleman, or even a member of the royal family, was a semi-public place. John Evelyn, the diarist, recorded how privileged he felt when he was invited by Charles II, along with a crowd of others, right into the bedroom of the king's mistress.

Here, at Bolsover, there was once a bed of purple velvet, with gold lace and embroidery 'worth £300 at least'. In another of William's houses, the bed was fenced off by a railing from the press of spectators.

DRESSING ROOM

There were some private rooms through the doorway (now blocked up) in the north-east corner of the room. Built in the 1660s, in the gap between the end of the Riding House Range and the Terrace Range, they consisted of a tiny stoolhouse – housing the 'close stool' or toilet – and a dressing room. The dressing room served an ulterior purpose – after receiving his guests in the lodging room, the occupant probably slipped out to a cosier bed in here.

Go through the doorway into the gallery.

The 'public' lodging room or bedchamber.

Here, in the lodging room, an important guest is listening to his steward reading out a letter while a servant helps him to dress

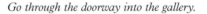

GALLERY

The gallery was originally even longer than it is now, measuring 140 feet before it was remodelled in the 1660s. The walls were lined with hangings, and there were 'Noble Chimney-Peeces of Blew and White Marble'. There was a painting called 'La Bataille Gaigne', showing William winning a battle and, later, another enormous painting of Bolsover Castle, both of which are now lost.

A contemporary painting of 1618 by Daniel Mytens, of Lord Arundel in his gallery at Arundel House. The gallery at Bolsover must have looked rather like this

RIGHT: One of the bizarre water spouts to be seen high on the wall of the Terrace Range

BELOW RIGHT: Sansovino's building for the Mint in Venice has pilasters constructed in a similar way to the ones on the Terrace Range, but the Venetian ones have bases in the traditional way. As well as showing the influences of the Renaissance on Bolsover, the comparison shows how bizarrely individualistic the Bolsover details are

NATIONAL PORTRAIT GALLERY

This room was used for walking, dancing and private conversation. It was a good place for members of the household to meet, as it was neutral in status, and not part of the hierarchy of formal rooms. Like the gallery of William's relative, Lord Arundel, at Arundel House in London, this room did not lead anywhere. The Arundel House gallery was one of the most fashionable in the country and one of the first to be used for displaying antique statues. The gallery at Bolsover perhaps had a similar artistic purpose, marking the change in style from the Elizabethan 'long gallery' to the 'sculpture gallery' or 'picture gallery'.

Turn left. The central arched doorway leads you outside, down a stone staircase and onto the Terrace, with its impressive panoramic view over the Derbyshire countryside.

TERRACE

If you walk over to the wall and turn to look back at the building, you will see one of Bolsover's most extraordinary features: the long west front of the Terrace Range. Centred on the staircase, the main section has a long series of large windows to light the gallery inside. Between the windows are its hallmark, the strange, fat pilasters, or half-columns, that resemble the barrels of cannons. This unusual creation was designed by John Smithson in the years before the Civil War, and is an impressive example of the early Mannerist style. There is a great diversity of detail in the architecture of this façade – from its medieval battlements and jutting water spouts to the boldly profiled classical pediments over the windows – but the combination works to create a striking overall effect. The cannon-shaped pilasters themselves are an eccentric interpretation of classical Ionic columns, with their spiral-scrolled capitals. Similar examples can be found in Italian palaces of the time and Smithson may have been familiar with them.

The pilasters also had a purpose connected with the development of the building. To the left, or north, you can see that the first four gables were originally a separate house. When the gallery was added, the windows of the basement were

SCALA ART RESOURCES

made higher as the builder moved south. The pilasters were applied not only to the Gallery, but also to the older frontage, to unify the effect.

THE SOUTH DRIVE

This dramatic driveway was originally the main approach to the Castle. Visitors could enter the Terrace Range via the stairs you have just descended, or up another flight, now missing. The foundations of the lost stairs are hidden beneath the grass, but the main doorway, originally leading into a passageway to the Great Hall, can be clearly seen, high in the wall.

VIEWPOINT

Charles Cavendish must have been very pleased with the site of his new castle as it had great potential to impress his neighbours. To the north lay Sheffield Castle and to the east, Worksop Manor, both his step-brother's houses. To the west lay Chatsworth, built by his mother and where he

had lived when young. To the south, and visible from Bolsover, lay the Halls at Hardwick, also built by the redoubtable Bess. Across the valley, also within sight, was Oldcotes, another house built by Bess of Hardwick, and next to it, Sutton Hall (now Sutton Scarsdale), completed by 1595 for Sir Francis Leake. According to folklore, Bess built Oldcotes (or Owlcotes as it was originally called), to rival Leake's Sutton Hall – it was to be 'as splendid for owls as his was for men'!

Bolsover faced boldly out over all this, and must have been conspicuous on its hilltop crest from many miles away. Bolsover's deer park began at the bottom of the slope, directly below the Terrace, and stretched down to meet Sir Francis Leake's deer park. The dividing line between the two was roughly where the motorway is now.

Today this outlook is completely different. Coal was worked here in William Cavendish's time and later exploited in deep mines, as the area became industrialised. The rows of terraced houses form a 'model village', built in 1894, to house the colliers.

Continue to the end of the Terrace and turn right up the steps into the courtyard of the Little Castle.

LEFT: The original main doorway to the Great Hall, high in the wall towards the north end of the Terrace Range façade

BELOW LEFT: A painting of Bess of Hardwick's Chatsworth by Richard Wilson, as it would have appeared in the seventeenth century

BELOW: The gallery entrance to the Terrace Range

THE LITTLE CASTLE

OPPOSITE: The Little Castle and the fountain garden from the south-east

You have now reached the oldest, most intimate and most unusual of the buildings at Bolsover. This was a separate house designed for retirement and extravagant pleasure. To enter this building is to leave the everyday behind, and to enter a new world where everything has a hidden meaning.

Standing in the courtyard with its high walls and turrets, you are in a miniature version of a medieval castle. Above the courtyard, with its fanciful arrow-loops, rises the compact tower with square form, corner turrets and battlements all purposefully reminiscent of a Norman keep. Bolsover's original fortified twelfth-century keep was indeed located near here, but the Cavendish castle was built for pleasure, not defence.

The courtiers of the early seventeenth century were obsessed with chivalry – they dressed up as medieval knights and took part in tournaments. The square forecourt of the Little Castle is the perfect stage-set for this type of play-acting.

Looking up at its façade however, you can also see more up-to-date continental influences. The classical balcony makes a sharp contrast with the surrounding medieval features and is of particular interest because we know an unusual amount about the likely source of its inspiration. In 1618, William Cavendish planned a trip to London to consider the 'furneshinge payntinge and carving' of his newly inherited house. He also sent John Smithson, his designer, to the capital to absorb the latest fashions in architecture and decor. There, Smithson sketched a number of details from London houses, showing the latest classical influences, including a doorway at Arundel House and a balcony from another house in the Strand. The doorway was designed by the architect Inigo Jones, who based his designs on Italian books and buildings. Smithson may have combined these two features in his design for the balcony doorway at Bolsover. It is also possible that he used the same pattern-books, (compilations of drawings for use by designers) as Inigo Jones. One in particular, by the fashionable Wendel Dietterlin, might have been used.

Smithson's drawing is all the more interesting because he has picked up neither the elegant balance of Jones's drawing, nor the intensity of Dietterlin's. Here, far from fashionable London, the simple presence of classicism was enough.

The iron balcony railing, one of the earliest surviving English pieces of such external ironwork, follows Smithson's drawing of the Strand house exactly, with its twisted, green-painted balusters and gilded ball finials. In the early seventeenth century, green paint was extremely expensive – railings would normally have been painted grey. Paint analysis showed

TOP: A design by John Smithson for the window inserted over the entrance to the Little Castle
MIDDLE: A design by Wendel Dietterlin from Architectura, *1598. BOTTOM: A design by Inigo Jones for a gateway at Lord Arundel's House in London, 1619*
LEFT: A drawing made by John Smithson of Colonel Sissell's house in the Strand in 1619

LITTLE CASTLE FLOOR PLANS

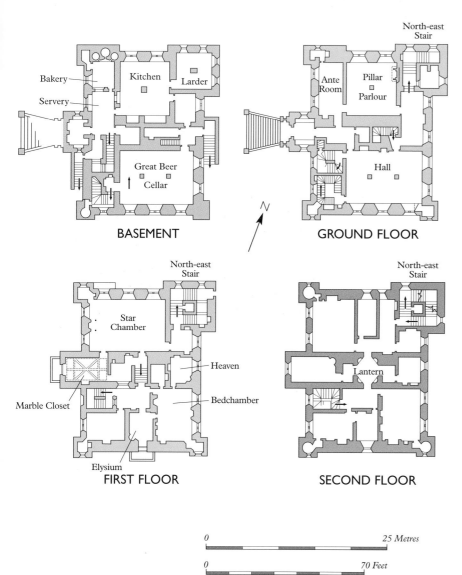

BASEMENT
- Bakery
- Servery
- Kitchen
- Larder
- Great Beer Cellar

GROUND FLOOR
- North-east Stair
- Ante Room
- Pillar Parlour
- Hall

FIRST FLOOR
- North-east Stair
- Star Chamber
- Heaven
- Marble Closet
- Bedchamber
- Elysium

SECOND FLOOR
- North-east Stair
- Lantern

0	25 Metres

0	70 Feet

Plans for the four floors of the Little Castle

RIGHT: One of the semi-circular wall paintings in the anteroom representing the melancholic temperament

that the original paint was indeed green with gilding, so the conserved ironwork has been repainted in green verdigris paint and regilded.

Beneath the balcony and over the main doorway, the stone-carved figure of Hercules supports the balcony's weight as Hercules supported the world. The original statue was heavily eroded and has been replaced with an accurately carved copy, as has the similar figure that overlooks the garden.

Once inside the Little Castle, turn into the small room immediately on your left.

ANTEROOM

This room may have been used for a porter or steward to greet guests.

The semi-circular wall paintings are a series of images copied from a set of prints after paintings by the Dutch artist Martin de Vos (1531–1603).

The paintings with figures illustrate three of the four Humours that were believed to govern the human temperament. They demonstrate the Renaissance idea that human beings fall into four types: the melancholic (symbolised by the old man and the girl over the door), the choleric or hot-tempered (the soldier and his mistress) and the phlegmatic or cool, and slow to anger (the fisherman and fishwife). One Humour, the sanguine, is mysteriously missing. It is thought that this was intentional, the witty implication being that the castle's owner, William Cavendish himself, represented the high-spirited, hot-blooded Humour. At the far end of the room is a painting depicting the Four Elements as an architectural arrangement. There are no figures in this picture, but if William stood below it, the sequence would be completed by his own presence!

Conservation of all the wall paintings was undertaken in the 1970s. While some areas suffered from major damage caused by water infiltration and structural movement, the majority of what can be seen is original.

Turn left out of the anteroom then right into the hall.

HALL

The room was originally designed to look like a plain stone room with a vaulted ceiling. In fact, the walls and ceiling vaults are finished with a stone-coloured plaster, incised to imitate blocks of stone. Since the seventeenth century the walls have been re-painted several times and the ceiling was overpainted in white. The panelling has now been redecorated in the original grey colour, and the ceiling has been repainted to match the original plaster.

ideas that William's refined and educated guests were used to having served up to them. Sight was considered to be the most ethereal sense, so appears first, and taste was the most vulgar. During Ben Jonson's masque, which was written and performed for King Charles I and his queen when they visited Bolsover in 1634, one scene discussed a similar 'Banquet of the Senses': 'When were the Senses in such order plac'd? The Sight, the Hearing, Smelling, Touching, Taste, All at one Banquet?'. It is quite possible that the king and queen may have partaken of a banquet of sweetmeats (desserts) in this very room, while the song of the senses was performed for them (see page 35).

The carved stonework of the room incorporates fruit and flowers, and winged horses. Its furnishings were originally sumptuous. At the time of William's death, it is known to have contained twelve cloth-of-silver chairs. The 'gothick' sash windows were inserted in the eighteenth century and double-glazed in the nineteenth.

Leave the Parlour and turn left up the stairs. As you pass the doorway onto the Stone Walk, pause and look down on the garden. The original door stands on the stairs. When you reach a doorway on the first floor, turn into another anteroom which leads to the Star Chamber.

THE FIREPLACES OF THE LITTLE CASTLE

The fireplaces of the Little Castle are one of its most unusual and attractive features. Mark Girouard, in his book about Robert Smythson, called them 'A series of completely original little masterpieces ...'

They are probably based on engravings by the famous Italian architect, Serlio, but are an extraordinarily inventive series of variations on a theme. All have great, stone-panelled hoods, and mix Gothic arches with extravagant classically-inspired ornament. Many are exquisitely carved in a variety of local English 'marbles' – pink alabaster, speckled cockleshell and black 'touch'.

A few of the black 'jewels' which adorn the fireplaces were missing. They have been replaced as part of the recent programme of conservation, after tracking down the source of the Ashford Black 'marble' to a mine on the nearby Chatsworth estate and reopening the mine for this purpose.

William Cavendish's second wife wrote a poem linking the fireplaces to love: 'chimneys of th'touchstone of affection made, Therein is beauty, as love's fuel, laid.'

The fireplace in the Pillar Parlour is particularly interesting because on the front it has William and his wife's coats-of-arms. On the round black 'jewels' set into the sides, William's crest (the serpent) and his wife's (the boar), unlike the coats-of-arms on the front, are topped with little crowns or coronets. This shows the fireplace must have been completed after 1620, the year in which William was made a Viscount, entitling him to add the coronet to his personal symbols.

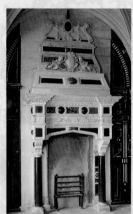

TOP LEFT: Smithson's design for the hall chimney
BELOW LEFT: The fireplace in the Elysium room.
TOP RIGHT: Pillar Parlour fireplace BELOW RIGHT: Drawing of a fireplace made by architect John James in the 1740s as a pattern for a fireplace at Welbeck Abbey

STAR CHAMBER

This is the 'Great Chamber' of the Little Castle. Only family and privileged guests would be allowed to ascend this far for meals or entertainment, while the household ate in the hall.

It is lavishly decorated, but would originally have appeared even richer, as the walls would have been hung with tapestry hangings: four 'peeces' were listed here in 1676. This is why a cheap, grey paint was used, and the effect, now that all of the panelling is exposed, seems rather dull. In the eighteenth century this problem was redressed by hanging a series of twelve paintings of Roman emperors and empresses from Welbeck Abbey here – copies of the famous series by the painter Titian. Later still, in the nineteenth century, these were joined by the Victorian tenants' collection of unusual objects.

The striking ceiling has been recreated to look as it would have done when it was first painted after the trip to London in 1618–19. Blue ceilings, resembling the heavens, were a common feature of royal palaces and chapels at this time. However, instead of the usual pigment, azurite (a crushed precious stone that was very expensive) the colour was achieved here using the cheaper

The Star Chamber, showing the newly-restored ceiling

Over the past ten years English Heritage has conducted a detailed examination of the interiors of the Little Castle. The Castle was already known to contain extremely rare seventeenth-century interiors, but recent research has established that they were probably some of the most refined and exquisitely decorated of the period. The decorative schemes chosen by William Cavendish clearly reflected the fashions current at the court of James I in about 1620. The interiors of King James's royal palaces have long since vanished, and the decorative schemes at Bolsover therefore offer a rare insight into the painted decorations of the period.

As the Little Castle was seldom used after the early eighteenth century, and as only minimal redecoration was carried out during the eighteenth and nineteenth centuries, much of the original panelling and decorative finishes still survived, worn but untouched, until the middle of the last century. However, in the 1970s, it was mistakenly assumed that the oak panelling would have been unpainted in the seventeenth century and that the surviving paint finishes were probably applied in

he nineteenth century. Therefore, in 1976, large areas of the wall panelling within the Little Castle were completely stripped and some of the original seventeenth-century decorative paintwork was overpainted using what today's conservators consider to be inappropriate colour schemes.

The programme of conservation, begun in 1999, aimed to conserve what remained of the original seventeenth-century decorative paintwork, and recreate the original scheme devised by William Cavendish. Detailed research involved the careful examination of John Smithson's drawings, early inventories, building accounts and photographs.

However, it was the evidence found within the Little Castle itself that provided the most important information about the exact nature of the original painted decoration. For example, the research established that the panelling in the Star Chamber had been strewn with smalt, a bright blue glassy pigment. Analysis of the painted schemes also provided a new understanding of later alterations and additions to the panelling, the placement of hangings and the original use of the rooms.

Where it was thought to be appropriate to recreate the lost paint finishes, authentic materials and techniques were used. All the paints applied were prepared and mixed on site by modern decorators in much the same way as they would have been in the seventeenth century, and some of the processes used have probably not been used by housepainters since then. The recreation of the original decorative scheme in the Pillar Parlour may claim to be the most accurate recreation of a seventeenth-century decorative scheme yet attempted.

Cross-section analysis of paint samples revealed that the original finishes on the green frieze of the Star Chamber, and much of the grained and stencilled panelling throughout the Little Castle, survived underneath the overpainting of the 1970s. Tests showed that it was possible to remove the modern paint to reveal the early finishes. Many layers of limewash that had been applied to the incised plaster in the passages and staircases was also carefully removed, to reveal the original stonelike appearance of the wallfaces.

Original stencilling emerges from behind later overpaint in recent work in the bedchamber

ABOVE: A cross-section of paint removed from the iron balcony of the Little Castle. The early green decorations can be seen at the bottom of the sample below the layers of later paint

FAR LEFT: Craftsmen laying out the gilded stars for the Star Chamber ceiling

CENTRE TOP: Removing excess smalt with a goose feather, before the application of the green glaze

LEFT: Mixing blue verditer in the basement of the Little Castle

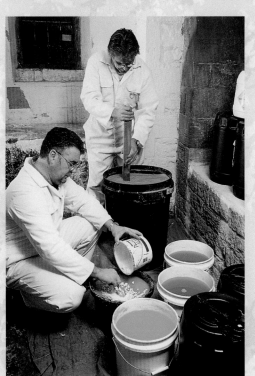

pigment blue verditer, which was a by-product of the silver refining process. This is its earliest known use. The stars are made of lead and gilded with gold leaf.

The heraldic devices on the frieze are the arms of Charles and William Cavendish and their wives Catherine Ogle and Elizabeth Bassett who both came from ancient families. Again, William was anxious to stress his connection with the older established families.

The panel paintings here, which depict both Old and New Testament figures, belong to a higher sphere than the mortals downstairs. The saints in the window reveals can be identified by the objects they hold: St Peter with his keys and St Catherine with her wheel. Saints Ursula and Catherine near the fireplace are actually modern copies, as their originals were stolen.

Between the windows are large panels showing King Solomon and King David, and in the north-east corner we can recognise Moses because he holds the Tablets of the Law. There are portraits of two elegant secular gentlemen in the north-west corner which could be of William and his brother Charles, still watching what goes on in their house.

The room contains another of the exquisite series of fireplaces. The decoration of this one was designed to remind guests that William Cavendish was related to the illustrious Gilbert, seventh Earl of Shrewsbury, as its front panel contains the arms of the Talbot family, with the Talbot dogs.

To the left of the fireplace, a door leads into a small but luxurious room.

ABOVE: A painted panel of two gentlemen in armour

CENTRE: The painting of Moses with the Tablets of the Law is dated 1621

BELOW: The front of the Star Chamber fireplace, depicting the Talbot coat-of-arms with its dogs. The fireplace has been repaired, but missing features such as the dogs' feet have not been replaced because of lack of evidence

RIGHT: One of the paintings of the Virtues in the Marble Closet. This one shows Fortitude with Patience who is crushing a heart in a press, to demonstrate that she can endure heart-ache patiently

MARBLE CLOSET

This was a 'closet' – an intimate room that could be kept warm and was usually used for conversation, playing cards or dressing. Margaret Cavendish, William's second wife, used hers for writing. A contemporary poet wrote of her room: 'Is this a lady closet? 't cannot be, For nothing here of vanity we see'

The newly-fashionable black-and-white marble from Italy was used instead of the coloured marble more popular in the sixteenth century, and a design was carefully sketched out beforehand by John Smithson.

Replicas of the original 'red taffetie' hangings have been recreated for this room, as, unlike most of the other rooms, there is enough information in an inventory of 1676 to judge what the hangings would have been like, and paint research has shown that the walls were not meant to be exposed. The inventory also tells us that the room had two backed chairs, two couches with red 'taffity quilts', a picture, two stands, a table and a looking glass. The areas of panelling not covered by the red hangings were decorated in a deep green glaze, produced using a very expensive and time-consuming process. The overall effect was very luxurious.

Unlike the lunettes downstairs, the paintings here are on canvas. They show a series of Virtues sitting in pastoral settings, after engravings by Hendrik Goltzius (1558–1617). But once again, two of them, Concord and Peace, are missing, as their place is taken by the window. Perhaps, again, the game was that a real person or people could fill the gap, and that during the royal visit, the king and queen were invited to stand on the balcony outside, presenting through the window the image of the two missing virtues with a real pastoral setting behind them. Many art historians describe the pictures in here without drawing attention to their risqué subject matter. Some feel that William had his own pleasurable uses for this room!

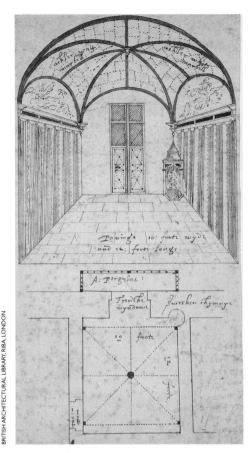

BRITISH ARCHITECTURAL LIBRARY, RIBA, LONDON

When the Castle fell to the Parliamentarians in 1645, this room was used by the wife of one of the soldiers as 'a spinning-room for toe and wooll'. What a come-down for its cavalier owner – his most private rooms had been invaded.

Return to the Star Chamber and leave it via the central door of the south wall to climb the short flight

of stairs to William's private suite of rooms which are arranged around an internal lobby. The decoration of these rooms, away from the public areas, is much more intimate, and only close friends of William would be invited to proceed on this last part of the journey through the Little Castle. Turn left into William's bedchamber.

BEDCHAMBER

Inside, the plain inner walls of the room would have been hung with expensive tapestries, while the panelling of the window wall was decorated with graining and delicate gold stencilling. This scheme was revealed in 1999 from beneath layers of modern grey paint.

With a roaring fire this would have been a cosy room. William's bed had a featherbed (mattress) and bolster, three blankets, a canvas quilt, a Holland quilt and a silk quilt. The tiny closet to the right of the fireplace was where the 'close-stool and pan' were kept. The stool was a seatless chair over a chamberpot.

Two closets lead from the bedchamber, each with a differently decorated door. The first, on the left of the fireplace depicts stories from Christ's life, while the other, Elysium, shows pagan gods and goddesses. The underlying idea is that in the Bedchamber the visitor is offered the path of virtue or the path of pleasure: divine love or physical love? Which should they choose? William was probably laughing at himself too – his guests would have been familiar with his reputation with women.

Enter the room to the left of the fireplace.

TOUR

LEFT: The design of the Marble Closet started as a drawing by John Smithson for the Elysium Room. It featured hangings and a marble ceiling

One of the fine stencilled decorations on the wall panelling in the bedchamber

The bedchamber

HEAVEN

This closet has a painted ceiling, dated 1619 over
the window, showing Christ's ascension to heaven,
and a painted frieze high up around the walls.
The weeping cherubs on the frieze carry the
instruments of Christ's crucifixion, while the
cherubs on the ceiling play music to celebrate his
ascension.

The paintings in both closets, like those
downstairs, are largely original, and their
remarkable survival makes them some of the
most significant wall paintings of their date in the
country. During the 1970s restoration, a few areas
of severe damage were repainted, such as the
frieze opposite the door in the Heaven Room. In
addition, all the wall paintings were varnished,
which has created a modern glossy appearance
that they would not have had originally.

In the corners of the ceiling are written
snatches of sheet music that come from a song
referring to Robin Hood. The significance was

that one of William's roles was to oversee
Sherwood Forest for the king. His other home,
Welbeck Abbey, was in the forest, and poets were
known to flatter him by calling him the 'Goodly
Oak of Sherwood'.

The decoration of the
panelling in this room may
be the earliest example of
seventeenth-century
chinoiserie. This Chinese
style decoration is painted
in shell gold, which is gold
leaf ground in gum and
stored in mussel shells. It
was thought to have been
400 times more expensive
even than gold leaf. The
cupboards would have held
precious artefacts.

*Return to the bedchamber and, through the door next
to the one you entered by, exit to the other closet.*

ELYSIUM

This closet, by contrast, depicts Elysium, the
heaven of the gods and goddesses of Ancient
Greece. The Olympians on the ceiling are copied
from the famous ceilings in the French palace of
Fontainebleau. The Olympian gods are denoted
by their symbols: Athena, goddess of wisdom,

has an owl; Diana, the huntress, has a moon; Juno, queen of the gods, has her peacock. The smith, Hephaestus, is using the net in the corner to trap his wife Venus with her lover Apollo.

The Elysium panelling has never been restored, and has a beautiful aged patina. It was made of oak, and retains traces of the original decorative scheme, which was very elaborate and costly. This is now extremely faded and worn. The panel beds were prepared with gesso, a mixture of chalk and glue, which was then polished before being glazed with indigo, and veined with gold, to imitate an exotic wood or marble.

The original French window is now blocked, but the balcony overlooks the fountain below which is surmounted by Venus, the goddess of love herself.

This is the end of the spiritual journey William has planned for his guests, and his final comment may be found above the window. This intriguing scene depicts a young boy (the figure on the right) pointing to another figure who holds an artist's palette and brushes. Between them, a painted banner carries the words: 'All is But vanite'. Though its full meaning is not clear, the scene

may be reminding the onlooker that the web of ideas presented throughout the Little Castle is in fact an illusion created by painting, and we, like this boy, can only look on and wonder. The irony of this message may be partly directed at William Cavendish himself, partly at his contemporary guests, and partly, whether he intended it or not, at the succeeding generations of visitors who have followed his spiritual guided tour.

Go back through the Star Chamber then ascend the next flight of stairs and you will come out into the 'Lantern'.

LEFT: Two figures over the window in the Elysium Room holding a banner with an implicit comment on the allegory of the Little Castle

BELOW LEFT: Bacchus, the god of wine, frolics with other Olympians in Elysium – the drops of wine can be seen dripping from the grapes he is squeezing

BELOW: The Elysium Room ceiling

LANTERN AND SECOND FLOOR

The unusual octagonal lantern provides light to the centre of the top storey of the house. The gold tint of the plaster gives the impression of perpetual sunlight. The space below it is rather like a miniature courtyard, and it would probably have been the hub of much activity. The niches in the walls were comfortable places to sit and talk.

The central space on the top floor of the Little Castle, lit by the lantern and its cupola

This third level contains rooms for members of the family and upper servants, used like bed-sitting rooms, and each probably sleeping several people.

The main staircase goes on right up to the flat leaded roof (inaccessible to visitors), which was used for walking about on in fine weather and watching the deer in the park.

Next, descend all the flights of the back stairs, down into the basement.

BASEMENT

This extensive basement housed kitchens, sculleries, a wine cellar and a bakehouse. The large room with the video has a stone floor with channels, because it was the 'great beer cellar.' The bakery still contains its ovens and there are several stone sinks. Meals were prepared here before being carried up any of the three staircases to the rooms above.

Leave the Little Castle by the staircase that leads you out into the Garden.

The bread ovens and sinks in the basement service area of the Little Castle

THE CASTLE OF LOVE

Having completed the journey through the Little Castle, we are in no doubt that the Little Castle was a house designed for, and about, love. Throughout the castle, William Cavendish plays with the various interpretations of love popular in his lifetime. The upward journey towards the Heaven room can be seen to mirror the neo-Platonist idea of the universe as a series of layers leading up towards God, which could be ascended by loving. However, we are soon convinced that William's principal preoccupation was a far more worldly kind of love.

The Castle is in a tradition of secret pleasure houses, such as the Palazzo del Té in Italy, built in the 1530s, by the Duke of Mantua, for his mistress. The Palazzo is similarly decorated and also features Hercules.

In many ways, the focus of the Castle is the Fountain Garden, which we have been encouraged to glimpse, tantalisingly, at intervals throughout our journey through the Castle. It is no accident, for instance, that the window of the Elysian room, the climax of the ascent through the castle, looks down onto the fountain below with its statue, Venus, the goddess of love.

The Garden provided the perfect setting, during the 1634 visit of King Charles I and his queen, for the masque specially written for them by Ben Jonson, *Love's Welcome* (see page 35).

Two cupids fighting over a palm, as they did in one scene of Love's Welcome, *the 1634 masque by Ben Jonson*

GARDEN

The garden combines the medieval idea of an enclosed, secret garden with the Renaissance idea of a garden as a place to display statues. The line of the Stone Walk is thought to lie on top of the remains of the medieval curtain wall, though its fabric is all seventeenth-century. There are many references in the 1612–13 building accounts to the demolition of the 'old Wall'.

The tunnel through the wall was originally further to the west, where one of the garden rooms is now. It was probably moved only when the Riding House was built, to create a straight line of view from the Riding House entrance through to the Little Castle.

The centre of the garden was simply lawn and paths, designed to be seen from the walk or windows above, which is why the fountain is set so deeply into the ground. The simplicity of the design was deliberate so that attention would focus on the sculptures.

The seventeenth-century appearance of the garden has been recreated as far as possible. The position of the paths was determined by archaeological investigation. The flower-beds are finished with a low hedge of wall-germander and wooden boards (this is where the word 'border' comes from). The actual layout of the plants

This garden, which has features in common with Bolsover, comes from Henry Hawkins's Partheneia Sacra, *1633, a book about the religious properties of gardens*

within the outer border is unknown, and their arrangement here is modern, but they are all species that were used in the seventeenth century, such as herbs and old varieties of roses.

One of the seventeenth-century drawings of Bolsover now at Renishaw Hall showing the Little Castle and the Fountain Garden

THE VENUS FOUNTAIN

The fountain combines the personal and bawdy with the elegant and classical. It is known to date from some time after 1628, because it has an earl's coronet on it, so belongs to the period after William became Earl of Newcastle.

The design drawing by John Smithson shows remarkable naked ladies sitting in the niches, squirting water. But an engraving of the fountain when first built in 1785, shows that the ladies had been replaced by busts of Roman emperors in white marble – a common theme for Elizabethan water features. Between the niches, on the round platforms, were four lustful beasts and four satyrs riding on birds who could be seen to be attacking the statue of Venus on the fountain's trunk.

TOP: John Smithson's initial design for the fountain, a very bawdy image of naked ladies using the fountain as a toilet

RIGHT: The Venus Fountain

BELOW: A carved griffin from the fountain

The quirky fountain is full of local character. Venus herself is copied from a slender and Mannerist original by Giambologna in Florence, but local carvers have used a picture of her and created quite a clumsy result. If Venus were to stand up, her legs would be of different lengths! She is made of a Derbyshire stone, as were the four black cupids.

The fountain has been painstakingly restored to recreate its original appearance as closely as possible and to make it play again. The design of the twenty-three new statues on the fountain was carefully researched from remaining marble fragments and historic pictures. The surviving fragments were of the beasts and satyrs. The emperors' heads were lost in the late nineteenth century, and the only image of them is an engraving by Rooke of 1785. Very unusually, the

emperors have no beards and are wearing pointed hats. Most seventeenth-century views show them with laurel wreaths. However, an 1893 list of books from the library at Welbeck Abbey included a book written in 1604 by Justus Sadeler, which could at least possibly have been there since the days of William Cavendish. Photographs were sent from America of the only known copy, and the emperors it showed wore hats, and had no beards like the ones on the Rooke engraving. It seems likely that these engravings were emulated in a comparatively unsophisticated manner by the original sculptors, and it has been the task of modern reconstruction artists and sculptors to work from these sources as the original craftsmen did.

The recreations of little boys and Caesars are castings, not black-and-white marble like the originals, but the satyrs and the fantastical beasts are new stone carvings to match the red-and-white limestone of the originals. Venus was lifted down and the trunk rebuilt, correcting a slant and incorporating new pipework. The statues were lifted into place, and the fountain plays again for the first time in two hundred years.

TOP: One of the emperors from Justus Sadeler's book, Caesars XII, *1604, a possible source for the masons who made the busts*

FAR LEFT: Part of a drawing of the Venus Fountain by Major Rooke, 1785, showing the Caesars' heads still in position

LEFT: One of the little boys on the fountain, reconstructed using the evidence from surviving fragments

WATERWORKS

The fountain today recycles its water by an electric pump. The way in which water was pumped up to the Castle in the seventeenth century is a fascinating study in itself.

There are various wells, but much of the water needed was pumped from across the valley. Engineers of the time were particulary interested in creating complex systems for pumping water to higher levels, turning wheels and working fountains.

The castle is the hub of a network of pipes, and four little 'conduit' houses, built in 1622, line one route, providing access

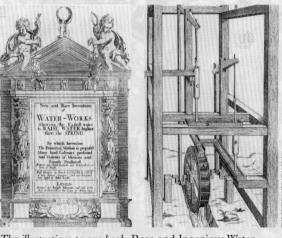

The illustrations to one book, Rare and Ingenious Water-Works, *show how water could be pumped to higher levels, turn wheels and work fountains. One of these new engineers probably advised William Cavendish on his sophisticated systems*

points for cleaning or pumping. The fountain was fed from the cistern house within the garden wall. This received water from the spring in the 'Cundy House' on the hill across the valley. The bottom chamber of the cistern house is at the same height as the spring, and the lead pipe linking them was only broken when the road in the valley was made eighty years ago. Once the water reached the cistern house, it was probably pumped up to the top-storey tank from where gravity could power the fountain. A final lead pipe went through the garden wall, across the lawn to the fountain.

2 John K: O'brans Pallas

THE HISTORY OF THE CASTLE

MEDIEVAL CASTLE

Before the Norman Conquest, Bolsover was in the Saxon kingdom of Mercia. In 1086, William the Conqueror granted the manor to William Peverel. By the twelfth century, there was a rudimentary castle at Bolsover as part of the fortification of the rocky ridge. The Peverels lost their Castle when they took the wrong side against the new king, Henry II, in 1152.

The Castle changed hands many times after that. It was usually held by the king and run by a constable appointed by him. In 1173, a £90 payment made partly at Bolsover, suggests that a keep was built. In the same year, £135 is recorded as having been spent on knights and their servants at Bolsover, Peveril and Nottingham Castles.

The remains of Peveril Castle at Castleton, also in Derbyshire and built by the same family, are the best clue to what the medieval castle at Bolsover would have looked like. It was a typical Norman keep, consisting of a stark, square tower, standing as a link in the chain of a curtain wall, with other towers at intervals. The keep is much smaller than the Little Castle, but it is the shape copied and romanticised by the seventeenth-century builders for this fantasy castle.

It is thought that the medieval curtain wall followed the line of what is now the fountain garden wall. The rooms hidden within the thickness of the wall at seemingly random intervals perhaps mark the position of the lost medieval towers. One tower was damaged in 1215 during a siege at Bolsover which was part of the barons' revolt against King John. Gerald de Furnival defended the castle for the king, while William de Ferrars, Earl of Derby, attacked for the barons. The castle garrison did not give up easily and one of the towers in the curtain wall was breached by the attackers. Its repair appears in the accounts for 1223.

This was the last medieval siege. After this, castles were built to impress as much as to defend. By the fourteenth century, Bolsover was let out to a series of custodians. It suffered 'waste

The shield appearing on the side of the fireplace in the Star Chamber links the arms of Gilbert Talbot and Mary Cavendish, to represent their marriage

Peveril Castle, also in Derbyshire, and also built by William Peverel. The medieval keep at Bolsover would have resembled this

OPPOSITE: Inigo Jones's design for a piece of stage scenery: 'The Palace of Oberon' (the fairy prince), from a masque performed at court in 1611. It shares many features with the Little Castle

LEFT: Part of a very unusual early drawing of Bolsover Castle that probably dates from the 1630s, and may be by the artist Kierincx, from Utrecht, who also worked for Charles I

OTHER 'MOCK' CASTLES

Many people think that Bolsover must be unique. In fact, it is the best, but not the only, example of a peculiar fashion for building little mock castles in the early seventeenth century. Jacobean aristocrats sometimes tired of life surrounded by their hordes of relatives and servants. They frequently had a secondary house or 'lodge', often architecturally more innovative than their main house, where they could retire with a small party. These sometimes took the form of play-castles where they could imagine that they were back in the age of chivalry.

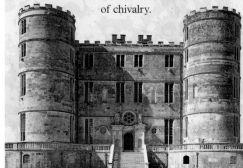

Lulworth Castle, in Dorset, completed in about 1607

and strip' as its materials were gradually sold off, and an Elizabethan traveller wrote disparagingly of it as 'a great building of an old castelle'.

CHARLES CAVENDISH AND THE BUILDING OF THE CASTLE

Charles Cavendish acquired Bolsover Castle from his step-brother and brother-in-law Gilbert Talbot, in 1608. He inherited from his mother an enthusiasm for building, and was described on his tomb, which lies in the special Cavendish chapel at the church near the castle, as a man whom 'wisdom, honour, content, made happy.' He was a soldier, but known amongst his friends as having a passion for architecture, music and the arts – all of which he passed on to his son William.

Charles probably chose the brilliant designer, Robert Smythson, to work with him on the design of his new castle. Although Smythson was now an old man, the Little Castle's clever planning and split levels, which were a hallmark of his work, make it seem likely that he was involved.

An almanack shows that the foundations for a new house had already begun early in 1613. Extensive accounts survive for Bolsover and we are therefore able to trace much of the progression of the building works in an unusual amount of detail.

The surviving accounts for 1612–14 show the carriage of stone and the construction of masons' lodges, as well as kilns to make the lime needed for mortar. The remains of the medieval castle were dismantled. Over fifty men were on site by 1614, and they were helped by many women, boys, and even girls. Some of the craftsmen had an official apprentice or 'boy', but many other children were employed casually in carrying stone and sand. All were overseen by 'Mr Smithson' (probably Robert's son John).

Bolsover Castle is a strange mixture of new and old ideas. Some features were taken from up-to-date houses in London, such as the curved 'Dutch' gables of the Terrace Range, which John Smithson sketched in 1618. But more often, books were used by masons for ideas, such as the engraving by Francini (opposite top), which was

RIGHT: Part of the original building accounts for the Little Castle, which include regular payments to 'Mr Smythson'

BELOW: Sir Charles Cavendish's tomb in the chapel which his son William had constructed in the church at Bolsover

used for the Riding House door. Identifying the sources is interesting, because as Francini's book did not come out until 1631, we can work out that the door could not have been designed before this. The work is sometimes seen as being imperfect and crude, because the Derbyshire masons were not trained in the classical style. Another view is that the distance from London actually enhanced the designs, because the craftsmen felt at liberty to put more creative interpretations onto their work. For example, the fireplace designs by Serlio were uniquely enhanced by the use of the local stone 'jewels' and family heraldic devices.

LIFE AT BOLSOVER

Charles Cavendish died in 1617, only four years after Bolsover was begun. After this, it served as one of the country homes of his son William until William's death in 1676. Welbeck Abbey was William's main home, but the household frequently visited Bolsover and used it for entertaining.

William had a household of forty-five people. The whole household, including William and his wife and five children, and all the staff, ate dinner together in the hall in the early afternoon, finishing at about 3 o'clock. A menu survives for the household at Welbeck and there were different tables for 'my lord', the steward, the gentlewomen, the children and nurses, the grooms, and 'those that wait on the masters'. The lower tables had only mutton and porridge, but William had larks, pies and 'other small boiled meat to furnish the table'.

The household contained a seamstress, the washer, a 'startcher' and a wardrobe man to look after William's splendid clothes, which were an important indicator of social status. William

wrote a series of little poems complaining about his servants: the butler grumbles, the wardrobe man steals the sheets and cushions, the groom of the Great Chamber spends all his time gambling, and the brewer waters down the ale until it is 'thin, & Naughtie'. The female members of the household are discussed very lewdly!

The business of managing the estate was supervised by William but he was helped in this by high-ranking servants such as secretary John Rolleston, chaplain Clement Ellis and steward Andrew Clayton. Clayton was finally dismissed for dishonesty, but his letters and his legal defence of himself reveal a lot about the running of the household.

LEFT: Above, an engraving by Francini, from his book Architecture, *1631, which was used in the design of the Riding House doors. Below, John Smithson's drawing of a new doorway for the Terrace Range*

THE SMYTHSONS

The main designers of Bolsover Castle were the famous Smythson family who worked with Charles and then with his son William. We usually know little about the lives of craftsmen at this period, but we know quite a lot about the Smythson family of masons. Originally from Westmorland, Robert Smythson was also involved with the design of many other fine houses, including Hardwick Hall, Longleat and Burton Agnes. The family was certainly involved at Bolsover, for plans survive connected to the Castle in the hand of John Smithson. John was the son of the more famous Robert, and held a position as an upper servant and estate surveyor under Charles and William Cavendish. He was addressed politely as 'Mr' Smithson, married into the minor gentry, and held land in Bolsover to farm.

The Smythsons were not architects as we understand them today. Although Robert was described on his tomb as 'architector and surveyor', he was essentially a mason with a flair for design, who worked in a team, and latterly he spent as much time on estate work and surveying as on designing. Both Robert (in 1609) and John (in 1618–19) had made trips to London to sketch the latest buildings. After John's death in 1634, a third generation of Smithsons became involved in finishing the works – John's son Huntingdon.

Another Smithson plan – this one for the basement of the Little Castle

William Cavendish in a copy, made in 1661, of an original portrait by Van Dyck who was a friend of William's

PRIVATE COLLECTION

WILLIAM CAVENDISH

William's tastes were formed early. From his father he inherited a love of music, poetry, architecture and swordsmanship. Even as a young man he squandered an inheritance on a singing boy, a dog and a horse, rather than sensibly buying land.

William was also known as an admirer of women, and, it would seem, a great philanderer. 'Whether this be so great a crime to condemn him', wrote his second wife, tactfully, 'I will leave to the judgement of young gallants and beautiful ladies'. He appears to have been a loving husband and wrote many love poems to both his wives as well as other women.

In 1618, he married Elizabeth Basset, a wealthy heiress from Staffordshire. He was forced to spend quite some time away from her and the children at court, but his affectionate letters home often say how much he was missing them.

Elizabeth became ill and died in 1643, while William was away fighting in the Civil War. In 1645 William met Margaret, who was to be his second wife, in Paris, at the exiled court of Queen Henrietta Maria.

Much of what we know about William is from a biography written by Margaret. She tells us that he wore fashionable clothes, unless they were

ABOVE: Elizabeth Bassett, William's first wife, painted at the time of her marriage to him in 1618 by William Larkin

RIGHT: Margaret shown in her closet with her writing table before her, in the frontispiece to her book The World's Olio, *1671 edition*

inconvenient for horse-riding and 'heroic actions' and that, 'He is neat and cleanly, which makes him to be somewhat long in dressing'. His attention to appearance was not so admired by those serving under him in the Civil War who complained that he 'lay in bed until eleven o'clock and combed till twelve'.

We also know from Margaret's biography that William ate little. He had only one meal a day, she said, 'at which he drinks but two good glasses of small-beer ... and a little glass of sack (sweet wine)'. He had sack for breakfast, with a 'morsel of bread' and for supper, 'an egg and a draught of small-beer'. Everyone drank beer in those days as water was not safe.

A proportion of William's time had to be spent in managing the estates, but even Margaret was forced to admit that he 'naturally loves not businesses, especially those of state, although he understands them as well as any'. He spent his time instead in music, poetry, architecture, and 'principally horses of all sorts, but more particularly horses of manage'.

William encouraged many professional poets, who in turn wrote poems praising him. In the 1630s, Mr Aglionby wrote of Bolsover that William would 'make thy mount, the Muses' Hill'. Some of William's plays were performed on the London stage.

MAD MADGE OF NEWCASTLE

William Cavendish's second wife, whom he called 'Peg', was known by the world as 'Mad Madge of Newcastle' for her philosophical books and outlandish behaviour. One contemporary felt

MARY EVANS PICTURE LIBRARY

'LOVE'S WELCOME'

King Charles had visited Sherwood Forest in 1633 and was 'royally feasted' by William Cavendish at Welbeck Abbey. The king was impressed, and asked if he could return the following year with his queen, Henrietta Maria. So, in 1634, William handed over Welbeck Abbey to the king and queen for several days in July. On the thirtieth of the month they came over to Bolsover, where a masque had been prepared for them. William had 'sent for all the gentry of the country to come and wait on their Majesties', and invited his friend Ben Jonson to write an entertainment called *Love's Welcome*.

The king and queen were treated to an unparalleled feast, which included peacocks, swans and sturgeon, and then the masque was performed. It was a string of scenes performed in different locations around the Castle. It possibly began in the Pillar Parlour where a tenor sang a song about the Five Senses,

while the king and queen ate a banquet, or small meal of sweetmeats. Then they retired to the garden, and were entertained with a speech by a 'surveyour', and a 'Dance of Mechanickes' including the carver, free-mason, plumber, glazier and mortar-man – presumably workmen who were still engaged on work on the Terrace Range.

After the dance, the king and queen had 'a second Banquet set downe before them from the Cloudes' by two cupids, which probably means that another dessert was lowered by a mechanical device from either the Elysium Room balcony, or from the high Stone Walk.

The Cupids then spoke flatteringly of the perfect love that existed between the royal pair, which is 'circular, and perfect': rather like the garden in which they sat. The whole entertainment cost nearly fifteen thousand pounds, a huge sum, intended to flatter the king into giving William a court appointment. After the king left however, William found himself 'plunged in debt' and gloomy about his prospects.

The extravagance and splendour of the occasion, where the tablecloths alone had cost £160, led one rather disapproving observer to call it a 'stupendous entertainment, which (God be thanked)... no man ever in those days imitated.'

CLOCKWISE FROM LEFT The first page of the text of Love's Welcome; *Charles I and his queen in masque costumes by Gerit von Honthurst; part of the list of 41 types of birds consumed during the royal visit to Bolsover in 1634; and a masquer from a court performance in a costume by Inigo Jones*

that 'that there are many soberer people in Bedlam.' She spent a lot of time writing in her closet, but she also liked to make striking public appearances. Pepys described her in her black velvet cap, her hair about her ears, naked-necked, and black patches covering up pimples. Another described her appearance in male attire saying that she wore a 'vest', and 'made a man's legs'.

Margaret's prolific writings were very unusual for a woman at this time. Her biography of William is fascinating both as a very human portait of him and of daily life at the time. Her love and respect for William seem to have known no bounds, but at the same time, she does manage to convey the private habits and foibles of a very public figure, including his diet, clothes

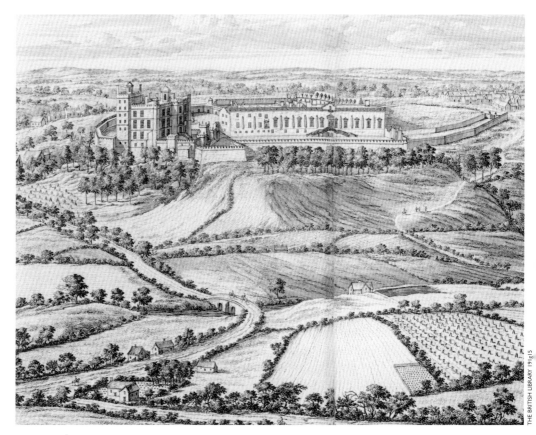

Part of Kip and Knyff's view of Bolsover Castle. John Holles, who married William's grand-daughter, commissioned it on 20 January, 1698

ABOVE: This illustration from one of Margaret's books shows an imaginary gathering of all William's children and their wives. In fact, as William was in exile, they never all met together

RIGHT: William Cavendish, in a plate from his book on horsemanship

and manners. She also wrote many other rambling and repetitive books; and believed that, as a Duchess, she should not have to revise her work for publication.

Elsewhere, she also discussed the inferior education and role allotted to women: but suffered the usual fate of women who did something well in a 'man's' field: her writings aroused an uneasy fear that the 'lesser' sex was overstepping the mark, and she was accused of dangerous peculiarity.

THE AMBITION OF WILLIAM CAVENDISH

William travelled to Italy as a young man with the English ambassador, Sir Henry Wotton. Here he found new ideas about elegant entertainment at the court of the Duke of Savoy. As an aspiring courtier, he understood that social standing could be maintained by etiquette: he wrote that 'ceremony, though it is nothing in itself, yet it does everything'. It was necessary that William's own household should

reflect the lifestyle of the court, and his country house at Bolsover was very important in this. In Sir Henry's words, the seventeenth-century Englishman's country house was to its owner, 'the Theatre of his Hospitality, the Seate of Self-fruition, the Comfortablest part of his own Life, a kind of private Princedom ... an Epitomy of the whole World'.

It is hard to imagine now how regimented and controlled courtly life was at this time. William's household, like a miniature version of the royal court, moved from Welbeck to Bolsover Castle and back, with all its trappings. William wrote a letter to Prince Charles, telling him to consider 'the cloth of estates, the distance people are with you, great officers, heralds, drums, trumpeters, rich coaches, rich furniture for horses, guards, marshal's men making room, disorders to be laboured by their staff of office, and cry, "now the King comes!"'

CIVIL WAR

William was a key Royalist leader in the Civil War as commander of the troops north of the Trent. Unfortunately he is famous for losing the north of England for the king in a crushing defeat at the Battle of Marston Moor in 1644. Following this he fled to the Continent to escape the Parliamentarian army.

In 1645 the Parliamentarians moved in on Bolsover Castle and began work on gun emplacements ready for bombardment. They were stopped before any damage was done by the 'coming of a Drum from the Castle for a Parley which concluded in Articles of Surrender'. Soon the 'Governour, Officers and Gentlemen' were allowed to march out 'with Drums and Colours, Horses, Swords and Pistols', but all their heavy guns and ammunition were taken. In 1653, parliamentary soldier George Hancock requested a pension from the government, for having been present at the rather unheroic 'taking of Bozer Castle'.

The castle proved to be a drain on the resources of the Parliamentary army and they discussed demolishing it, so that neither side could use it, and orders were finally given for this in 1649. The house was not to be damaged, but it was requested that the 'outworks abroad, and garden walls, with the turrets and walls of the frontier court that are of strength, be demolished, and all the doors of the house be taken away and slight ones set in their place'.

The Castle was sold to a speculator called Robert Thorpe for the value of its materials. William couldn't return to England unless he 'compounded', or apologised to the government for his role in the Civil War, which he wouldn't do. Fortunately, his brother, the second Charles Cavendish, stepped in. Charles very generously 'compounded' himself, paying a fine as a punishment, and then bought back the family estates, handing them over to William's children so that they could use the income.

RE-BUILDING AFTER THE WARS

William Cavendish was delighted when, in 1660, with Oliver Cromwell dead and no-one else seeming strong enough to take his place, King Charles II was invited to come home again. William had been living lavishly in Antwerp, in the house of the painter Rubens, as a great nobleman was expected to, but without the income from his estates. Now he expected his loyalty to be rewarded.

However, in the short term, William was disappointed. The king's new advisers thought him 'a very lamentable man'. He was never quite able to shake off the disaster of Marston Moor; his reputation for retiring to 'sweet company' instead of running his army; or of going abroad instead of rallying his men. A pamphleteer used this, and his fondness for writing plays, to make him a figure of fun: 'But the Earl

Oliver Cromwell, the Parliamentarian leader in the Civil War

A nineteenth-century painting by Abraham Cooper of the Battle of Marston Moor which William Cavendish lost for the Royalists

of Newcastle, the brave Marquess of Newcastle, which made the fine plays, he danced so quaintly, played his part a while in the North, was soundly beaten, shew'd a pair of heels, and exit Newcastle.'

Unable to afford a good house in London, William was forced to return, with Margaret, to Welbeck and the 'naked house' at Bolsover.

However, Charles II did not completely forget his old tutor, and in 1665 he granted William the new rank of Duke. The grandson of a sheep farmer had received the highest honour.

William now set to work to restore the family home at Bolsover. A flurry of letters survive, between William, his steward Andrew Clayton, his overseer Samuel Marsh and the contractor Joseph Jackson, about the progress of repairs. New lead was bought for the gallery roof and repairs were carried out to the Stone Walk, which had lost its battlements. A whole new suite of state rooms was built at the south-eastern end of the Terrace Range and the Riding House range was repaired. The grand gateways into the castle, and the grand staircase from the gallery to the terrace also date from this period.

William died on Christmas Day, 1676, aged 83. He was buried in Westminster Abbey, under a tomb marked 'The Loyall Duke'. William's dukedom died with his son Henry in 1691. The Castle passed three times through the female line in the eighteenth century: through Henry's daughter, and then his grand-daughter, to the Earl of Oxford, and again through his daughter

The main doorway to the new state rooms added to the Terrace Range by William Cavendish in the 1660s

to the Duke of Portland. The Dukes of Portland remained the Castle's guardians until 1945 when it was given to the nation.

EIGHTEENTH-CENTURY BOLSOVER

The eighteenth-century accounts do not show a completely abandoned house. The Countess of Oxford added the pointed 'gothick' windows to the Pillar Parlour in the Little Castle. There was careful and continued maintenance under the Dukes of Portland: the third Duke visited to see his horses, which were kept in the Castle Yard.

However, the Castle was summed up by an eighteenth-century guidebook writer, Samual Bray, as 'ill-contrived and inconvenient' and tales are told locally of its being plundered for building materials and furniture. Building materials were taken from Bolsover to be used at Welbeck in the 1740s, and later the lead roof from the Terrace Range was also taken.

Another tradition, recorded in 1852, told of 'a great sale at Bolsover, which lasted ten days, when crowds of purchasers came from all the neighbouring counties...'.

Again, many of these items ended up at Welbeck, such as the many pictures known to have hung in the Terrace Range. Other items that have disappeared are the crimson velvet chairs (mentioned 1657); the mahogany dumb-waiters (1750) from the Pillar Parlour; 'tea aequipage' in the Marble Closet (1754), the 'Noble Chimney-Peeces of Blew and White Marble' from the Gallery (1710), and the stalls from the huge stable.

Tourists began visiting Bolsover in the late eighteenth century. The first notable visitor was

The Castle depicted by Nathaniel and Samuel Buck, 1727, showing the battlements along the terrace which were lost and only recently replaced

James Byng, an irrepressible diarist who stole brasses from the church in the next parish before visiting Bolsover in 1789. Surprisingly, Bolsover did not impress him as a ruin. He thought, prosaically, that it would make a good school, 'which shou'd allways be done with these old houses'.

NINETEENTH-CENTURY BOLSOVER

In 1828, the Reverend Hamilton Gray, curate and later Vicar of Bolsover, moved into the Little Castle, having forced his drunken predecessor, the Reverend Tinsley, to leave.

He and his wife found 'the most dismal desolation, wainscots torn down, windows rattling in every pane, doors off their hinges ... the numerous staircases were whitewashed like barracks, the pictures which had covered this nakedness were without frames, often shot through with arrows'. But they set to work to convert it into a Victorian country house, complete with kitchen garden and greenhouses. A now-vanished porch was cut into the south wall of the castle, some of the wall panelling was moved about, and trees began to blur the silhouette of the Castle.

The Reverend and Mrs Gray were very snobbish and intensely proud of their acquisition. Reverend Gray boasted, 'You will not find monumental chimney-pieces, frescoed walls, arched cupolas and a marble boudoir in other parsonages'. They complained of never breaching the social defences of their landlord, the fourth Duke of Portland. The Duke repossessed his Castle for his eighty-first birthday in 1849, when two thousand guests filled the terraces in an occasion as splendid as the royal visit of 1634.

Unlike eighteenth-century visitors and inhabitants, the Victorians, with their sentimental love of 'Olden Time' attached great value to this castle. They loved anything Elizabethan or Jacobean and therefore Bolsover was their ideal. However, the nature of some of the wall and ceiling paintings was apt to offend Victorian sensibilities. The room known as 'Elysium', with its naked gods and goddesses, was known as 'Hell' by the Grays and its subjects described as 'blood-curdling, Satanic themes'.

The Grays had eclectic tastes. The Star Chamber was crammed with a Victorian compendium of 'Grecian vases .... Scaraboei or Gem Beetles in onyx' and a 'collection of relics of the Stuart princes, consisting of objects which were the property of Mary, Queen of Scots, Charles Edward, and Cardinal York'.

Views of Bolsover appeared in Nash's *Mansions of England in the Olden Time*, and even in novels, such as a serialisation in the British Churchman about William Cavendish's royal cousin, Arbella Stuart. Anachronistically transported to Bolsover Castle, she was found by her lover sitting in the Star Chamber and listening to

DERBYSHIRE LOCAL STUDIES LIBRARY

The Castle illustrated in the Mirror of Literature, Amusement and Instruction *in 1832*

LEFT: *The Reverend John Hamilton Gray, tenant of the Little Castle from 1829*

A group of nineteenth-century visitors stand in front of the Terrace Range

'the genii of Bolsover, in the wild and fitful blasts, which do reign in this castle ...'. The Grays welcomed many visitors in search of Arbella's 'thick and wild fancies'. They also received the British Archaeological Association, and Sunday School sports in the grounds. Visitors were invited to leave their mark, for cut into the lead roof of one of the courtyard lodges was a collection of 140 outlines of tiny feet, many showing the symmetrical outline of shoes before left and right were introduced in the 1830s.

TWENTIETH-CENTURY BOLSOVER

Queen Mary visited Bolsover in 1912, and made a tour of the now-asphalted Stone Walk. In the 1950s the artist John Piper visited with the author Sacheverell Sitwell. Piper loved to draw ruins and made some haunting depictions of Bolsover. Sitwell wrote of the Castle's 'ghostly fire of the imagination, that can never be forgotten, and that never cools'.

Some light was shed on the First World War history of the Castle in 1995 when archaeologists found a bullet embedded in the Gallery wall, in the Terrace Range. The experts were puzzled at first, because although Bolsover did fall to the Parliamentarian enemy in 1645, and was 'well-manned with soldiers' and 'strengthened with great guns', contemporary accounts do not record a single shot being fired. The mystery was solved when they found out that during the First World War, the gallery had been used as a rifle range.

In 1945, the site was handed over to the Ministry of Works. It was opened to tourists from 9.30 am to 7pm, and postcards were on sale.

Extensive heavy engineering work was begun at this time to save the Little Castle from slipping down the rocky hillside. In the 1970s, the building had to be pinned from wall to wall with long steel rods, while an invisible concrete ring-beam was built around the Riding House, which had been on the verge of collapse.

In the 1990s, a long programme of stone repair and replacement was completed, as Bolsover's stonework had suffered badly from industrial pollution. The interiors of the Little Castle have been extensively conserved and restored as described on the preceding pages, while in the garden below, the renewed fountain plays over its statues.

Turn-of-the-century postcards of Bolsover Castle

RIGHT TOP: The inhabitants of Bolsover host a rifle practice in the Gallery during the First World War

RIGHT: The Terrace Range, painted by John Piper in the 1940s